THE HANUKKAH BOOK

MARILYN BURNS

illustrations by

MARTHA WESTON

FOUR WINDS PRESS   NEW YORK

Also by Marilyn Burns

THE I HATE MATHEMATICS! BOOK
THE BOOK OF THINK
I AM NOT A SHORT ADULT
GOOD FOR ME!
THIS BOOK IS ABOUT TIME
GOOD TIMES

Library of Congress Cataloging in Publication Data
Burns, Marilyn.
The Hanukkah book.

Summary: Discusses why and how Hanukkah
is celebrated and includes recipes, songs,
and instructions for playing with a dreidel.
1. Hanukkah (Feast of Lights)—Juvenile literature.
[1. Hanukkah (Feast of Lights)]   I. Weston, Martha.
II. Title.
BM695.H3B87   296-4'35   80-27935
ISBN 0-02-716140-4   AACR1

Four Winds Press
Macmillan Publishing Company
866 Third Avenue, New York, NY 10022
Collier Macmillan Canada, Inc.

Printed in the United States of America
First Edition
10 9 8 7 6 5 4 3 2

Special thanks go to the children who so willingly
shared their Hanukkah feelings:
Susie Blau, Bob Blumenfield, Jay Blumenfield,
Sharon Blumenfield, Jennifer Borkon, Rachel Broudy,
Elizabeth Burns, Jason Burns, Jay Gottfried,
Gary Hirschhorn, Larry Hirschhorn, Lisa Kolb,
Eve Larner, Lisa Levin, Leila Mead, Murray Moore,
Serina Moore, Lynn Rabin, Sara Roseman,
Jonathan Rosen, and Joan Singer.

CONTENTS

◆

INTRODUCTION

Hanukkah is the Hebrew word for "dedication," and the celebration of Hanukkah is often called the Festival of Dedication. It's an exciting holiday, filled with eating special foods, singing songs, playing games, and giving and receiving gifts. Hanukkah is a joyful time, one that isn't meant to interrupt work or any other part of life. It's a holiday when the main focus is celebration, not religious prayer. It's a time for people to come together to retell the Hanukkah story and have a good time. This is a book about all that Hanukkah is, for kids who want to know.

WHAT YOU'LL LEARN

This book has three purposes. They don't appear separately, but are woven into all the chapters. They're not too hard to pick out once you know about them.

One purpose of the book is to give you a source of information about Hanukkah. This includes the story of the struggle that led up to the first celebration of this holiday. It includes information about many of the traditions that have grown for celebrating Hanukkah—how to light the candles, what blessings are said at that time, what foods have come to be special. You'll learn why Hanukkah moves around in December, starting on different dates each year. You'll learn the rules for playing dreidel. Hanukkah songs are included as well.

The second purpose of the book is to take the basic traditions farther, to get you doing as well as reading about Hanukkah. The standard traditions are here as well as suggestions that may be new to you. You'll learn a variety of ways to celebrate. There are directions for making your own candles and Hanukkah menorahs. There are recipes for making special foods for a Hanukkah celebration. There are ideas for presents you can make.

The third purpose is to help you explore how you feel about Hanukkah. This has to do with what is inside your own head and heart. Some ideas to get you thinking are wedged into the book here and there—ideas about how other kids feel about Hanukkah and celebrate it with their families, about the place of Christmas in the lives of Jews, about how traditions grow and change. Hopefully, this book will get you thinking about the significance of this celebration, especially to you in your life.

DON'T PUT HANUKKAH IN A SPELLING BEE

How Hanukkah is spelled in this book is just one choice of several possibilities. There's no one right way to spell Hanukkah in English. That's because it's a Hebrew word. The Hebrew alphabet is very different from the alphabet used to write English words. Written in Hebrew, Hanukkah looks like this: חנוכה. There's no way to read that unless you can read Hebrew.

What's been done in English is to try and spell Hanukkah as it might sound if spelled using our alphabet. There's a word that describes doing just that—it's called transliteration. That usually helps. But there's a basic problem here.

The beginning sound of Hanukkah is a sound that is used in Hebrew but isn't used in English. There's really no way to spell it. It's like an "H," but starts further back in your throat. You make it sort of by clearing your throat at the same time you start to say the word. That's why some people spell Hanukkah with a "Ch" at the beginning: Chanukah. That seems to give the idea that there's more to the beginning sound that just the "H" tells.

Then there's disagreement about whether it should be spelled with two "n's" and one "k," or the other way around, or with or without the final "h." So you may see it spelled any of these ways: Hanukkah, Chanukah, Hanukah, Channukah, Hannukah, Chanukkah, Chanuka. You probably won't see it spelled like either of these: Hannukkah or Channukkah. But then you never can tell. In any case the choice is yours.

THE STORY OF HANUKKAH

One day in the year 332 B.C.E. (Before the Common Era), Alexander the Great marched into Jerusalem. The young Greek king had defeated the Persian armies just two years earlier. That victory had given him control over all that the Persians had ruled. This empire included Judea, the land of the Jews, the land with Jerusalem as its capital city.

Much to Alexander's surprise, his soldiers met no resistance in Jerusalem. Quite the opposite! The Jewish High Priest came with a procession to greet him. Alexander was pleased by this welcome. He proved to be a tolerant leader, who allowed the Jews to govern themselves in many ways. He allowed them to observe their religious laws and he did not insist that young Jewish men join his army. For their part, the Jews declared that they would name all male babies born in the first year of his reign Alexander.

The Jews were used to being ruled by foreigners. The change in power from the Persians to the Greeks seemed to mean that taxes were ultimately paid to someone else, little more. The actual collecting of the taxes, as well as other governing tasks over Judea, were carried out by the Jewish High Priest in Jerusalem and Alexander did not interfere with this practice.

The Temple in Jerusalem was the seat of the High Priest's governing. It was the most important building in Jerusalem and in all of Judea. More than a governing institution, it was a visible reminder of God's presence and a source of great pride. Especially in the face of foreign rule, the Temple was a unifying bond for all Jews.

Farmers who lived in Jerusalem or in the small villages that surrounded the city's walls came to the Temple to offer sacrifices to God. With the city's artisans and merchants, they gathered at the Temple, maintaining the strength of their religious beliefs. The change from Persian rule to Alexander's leadership didn't change their day-to-day existence, or their reverence for their religion, at least not right away.

But Alexander had a dream of how the world might be under his rule. He wanted to do more than just receive taxes from conquered peoples. He wanted to spread the Greek way of life everywhere. It was fine for people to govern themselves and, for now, to observe their own ways of life. But Alexander wanted to unite eventually all people into one culture, the Greek culture. He wanted them to learn the Greek language, and to study Greek philosophy, science, and art. Alexander planned to do this by encouraging his soldiers to move into various parts of his empire. They would live with the people there, marry and start families. In time, the soldiers would help the people learn about Greek customs and Greek thought.

The Jews were not excluded from Alexander's dream. But to Jews, learning about Greek ways posed no major problem. It was interesting to study new ideas, to learn a new language and customs. Besides, Jews were still able to live their lives by their own religious beliefs, following the Law of the Torah.

Does that seem so different than it is today in the United States? The government and many of the national customs and holidays have little to do with being Jewish. But it is possible to live as a Jew here today, and, at the same time, enjoy being an American. Thanksgiving and July 4th aren't Jewish celebrations, but ones that Jews can enjoy. Pizza, chow mein, and tacos aren't Jewish foods, but lots of Jews find them tasty. In Judea at the time of Alexander's rule, parts of life were lived the Greek way; and, for Jews, parts of life were lived the Jewish way. You can look at it as a sharing of two worlds.

When Alexander died after only twelve years in office, quarrels over power erupted among his generals, Ptolemy and Seleucus. They divided the empire, with Ptolemy taking Egypt and Seleucus taking Syria and Asia Minor. But they both wanted control of Judea. Ptolemy won. He did this by entering and seizing Jerusalem. He marched into the city on a Saturday and was astonished when the Jews made no effort to defend themselves. The Greeks did not understand the idea of Sabbath, and thought the Jews were foolish people.

The kings who succeeded Ptolemy generally believed in "live and let live." For more than a century, Jews continued to pay their taxes to the Ptolemic leaders while maintaining their own self-government under their High Priest. Jews also kept up their own cultural and religious practices, while learning more and more of the Greek ways. This learning continued to be encouraged by the Greek rulers over time. Their goal was hellenization—the total acceptance of the Greek customs, ideals, and language by all people. The Greeks didn't force this, but they tried to introduce their own ways into daily life, mainly by encouraging Greeks to move in and settle among other people.

SOME JEWS BEGIN TO CHANGE

Over time, some Jews did become hellenized, moving farther and farther away from Jewish customs and laws. For some this happened because they moved to farms or cities outside of Judea, but even in the land of the Jews, changes took place. More Jews wore the Greek-style tunic. Some took Greek names for social or business reasons. Synagogues were built that resembled Grecian temples.

Religious beliefs began to change. The attitude among some Jews was this: Why should we cling to our different ways? Why not be like all others? In Judea, this attitude was felt especially by those Jews who came into daily contact with people living the Greek way. Most of these Jews lived in the city of Jerusalem and were from the wealthier families. They generally were merchants who had a great deal of contact with people other than Jews. These Jews claimed they did not really want to give up Judaism, but they wanted to make Jews more like Greeks so that people who lived in cities neighboring Judea would look upon Jews as people just like themselves.

While some Jews felt this way, others were horrified by these changes in attitude. "It's not possible to live in two worlds," they said. "Hellenization is a threat to the future of the Jewish people." An undercurrent of unrest developed between those Jews who feared and resisted hellenization and those who felt it was backward and unrealistic, as well as undesirable, to resist Greek life.

Think about life today in the United States. Jews live as Jews in many ways. Some have given up many of the traditions of Jewish life. You can't say they've been hellenized, because their ways aren't Greek. Maybe you could say they've been Americanized. But then, there are Jews who are proud to be

Americans, who also make their Jewish heritage a significant part of their daily lives. There are lots of ways to be Jewish today, as there were then.

THE RULE CHANGES AGAIN

Along with this growing struggle among the Jews, another struggle was developing. This was between the Ptolemies (who ruled Egypt and Judea), and the Seleucids (who ruled Syria and Asia Minor). Though Seleucus had been content to concede the control of Judea to Ptolemy, his descendants wanted to rule that territory. About 125 years after Alexander had died, a Seleucid king finally did force the Ptolemic rulers to give up control of Judea. This Syrian king was named Antiochus III.

Antiochus III made energetic attempts to hellenize people, requiring that everyone put statues of himself and the Greek gods in prominent places. To erect such statues, especially in the Temple in Jerusalem and in synagogues throughout Judea, was unthinkable to the Jews. They claimed that paying taxes was enough proof of being good citizens. Antiochus III did not insist. Neither did his successor, his son Seleucus IV.

But the next leader was Antiochus IV, a man who called himself Antiochus Epiphanes. This meant "the visible god." Among Jews he became known as Antiochus Epimanes—"the madman." He wanted to extend his power and capture all of Egypt. In order to do that, he needed the full support of all the people under his rule. To him, that meant that the people had to become, once and for all, totally hellenized: They must speak Greek, follow Greek customs, worship Greek gods, and even think like Greeks. The Jews were especially important to him since Judea bordered on Egypt.

Those Jews who were willing to be hellenized thought it would be to their advantage to help Antiochus hellenize the rest of the Jews. Some of them convinced Antiochus to appoint a High Priest who would help. They recommended a man who had already adopted many Greek ways. He'd even changed his name from Joshua to Jason. As High Priest, he was not only to govern the Jews; he was to make sure they were becoming hellenized as well.

Under Jason's rule, statues of Greek gods were put up in the Temple in Jerusalem, Jewish priests officiated at Greek rites, and Greek athletic games were held in the Temple courtyards. But Jason also allowed Jews who wanted to preserve their own religious ways to do so. This leniency troubled those Jews who were anxious for hellenization and some of them complained to Antiochus. They even offered the king money if he'd appoint a new High Priest, one who would be stricter. And so, although Jason had caused more hellenization in twelve months of lenient rule than had happened in all the years since Alexander's death, he was removed from office and forced to flee.

Menelaus was appointed. He was a Jew who was not even a member of a high priestly family, and he cared less for the Jewish way of life than he did for his own power. There wasn't enough money in the Temple treasury to pay Antiochus the sum that he'd been promised for appointing Menelaus. Menelaus' solution was merely to sell some of the holy vessels of the Temple to raise the money that was needed!

THE JEWS FINALLY REVOLT

While the hellenization efforts were being supported by some Jews, unrest from other Jews continued to grow. Some of the anti-hellenizers organized into a group called the Hasideans. This group was deeply troubled and angered about the hellenization, especially at the Jews who had chosen Jason, and then had him replaced by Menelaus. The Hasideans grew in strength, and they planned to revolt as soon as it was possible.

Their time came. Antiochus, feeling secure that the hellenization was progressing well, had gone off to Egypt with his Syrian army to challenge the Romans who were now in control there. News that Antiochus had been killed in battle came back to Jerusalem. When the Hasideans heard this, they attacked Menelaus' supporters at the Temple. None survived. The Hasideans threw all the Greek statues over the Temple walls. And then they killed every known hellenizer they could find, and took control of the city. Even though Menelaus was away from Jerusalem at the time, it was an effective massacre.

But there was one big problem. The news of Antiochus' death had been just a rumor. He was alive. While in Egypt, he had lost his battle against the Romans. The Romans had spared his life, but had shamed and humiliated him, making him promise never to attack again. So Antiochus was very much living when he returned to Jerusalem, sulking from his defeat. When he found out about the Hasidean revolt, he was infuriated. He marched his armies into Jerusalem, where they senselessly killed 10,000 people. Their victims were not only Hasideans and Hasidean supporters; hellenized Jews and their families were slaughtered as well. The bloody punishment didn't stop.

Antiochus attacked the Temple. He removed the altar, the furniture, and the treasures. New Greek statues were installed.

To the Jews, this was a dreadful sign. Antiochus went further. He decreed that Jews could not observe the Sabbath, study the Torah, or circumcise their sons, under penalty of death. If a circumcised baby was found, he was hung around his mother's neck and both were thrown over the city walls, along with anyone who had participated in the circumcision. Soldiers broke into homes looking for signs of Jewish life. If they found any evidence, they would pronounce those people enemies and kill them. It was a nightmare to be a Jew in Jerusalem at that time.

Jews reacted in different ways to this terror. Some felt that the only thing they could do was to go along with the Greek rule. Others, who had been Greek supporters, were so filled with grief and rage that they switched their loyalties to the Hasideans and the cause of religious freedom.

Many families left Jerusalem, fleeing to smaller villages where they hoped to live simpler and more peaceful lives. That didn't work. Antiochus sent his patrols to villages, calling together the Jews, and demanding they make sacrifices to show allegiance to the Greek way. Refusal meant death. In some villages, Jews went along with the sacrifices, feeling it was more important to live than to die for breaking a Jewish law. In some villages, Jews refused and were tortured and killed.

In the year 168 B.C.E., a patrol of soldiers entered Modi'in, a small village located in the countryside to the northwest of Jerusalem. They went to the central marketplace of the town where they erected an altar. The soldiers then assembled all the men of the town. The priest and elder of Modi'in, Mattathias, was among them.

A descendant of the revered Hasmonean family of priestly Jews, Mattathias stood with his fellow townsmen, along with his five sons: Jonathan, Simon, Judah, Eleazar, and John. The soldiers led forth a pig, which they had brought with them, and asked who was the most respected among the villagers. Mattathias was identified.

The commander of the patrol addressed him. "Step forward," he ordered, "kill the pig, eat some of its flesh, and you and your sons will be considered friends of the king." Mattathias did not move. He knew that making the sacrifice would be an act of honoring the Greek gods as well as disobeying the Jewish dietary law. He knew that if he made the sacrifice, each of the other Jews would also have to eat the meat or be executed. Mattathias' choice was clear. "We will not obey the law of the king by departing from our worship," he answered.

There was a tense silence while everyone waited to see what would happen next. Another Jew was the one to break that stillness. "I will do as you bid," he said to the commander. "I will follow the king's orders." He approached the animal. The soldiers stood at attention next to the altar while the Jews watched hopelessly. Mattathias could not control his rage. Suddenly he rushed forward, snatched the commander's sword, and killed his fellow Jew. And then he turned on the commander and killed him too. The force of his action spurred his sons and the other villagers to attack. The soldiers had no time to collect themselves. They were all killed.

This was not a joyous occasion for the villagers. They knew that when the patrol didn't return to headquarters, another would be sent to investigate. They had to flee. "Follow me," Mattathias cried to the others. "Every one of you who is zealous for the Law and supports the covenant, come with me." His sons and other supporters took as much of their own food and equipment as they could. And they took their farm animals and weapons of the dead soldiers. But they left much behind—all the comforts of their homes, many of the family remembrances they treasured, and the life they knew in the village. They could make no other choice: They feared the power of Antiochus and his army.

THE JEWISH FORCES ORGANIZE

Mattathias fled with his followers to the mountains where they felt they could hide easily. No army was sent to track them down. Maybe it seemed unlikely that they could make any more trouble. Maybe it was because the Jews of the village of Modi'in weren't important leaders or well recognized in Jerusalem. Whatever the reason, it was a big mistake for Antiochus.

In the first year spent organizing to fight, Mattathias' group of people expanded. Some of the Hasideans joined them. They went to many villages, undoing what Antiochus' men had done. They tore down the Greek altars and circumcised all the uncircumcised boys, often by force. Many Jews greatly feared Antiochus and his Syrian army. Others had been hellenized. But Mattathias and his followers demanded obedience from all Jews to the Laws of Moses.

With persistent effort, Mattathias found and trained recruits and expanded his force. During that first year, this small band of Jews would strike out from time to time at a Syrian patrol, or disrupt ceremonies the Syrians were trying to hold in other villages.

The aged Mattathias never lived to see the outcome of his resistance. He died during that first year. But the revered priest and fighter helped make a vital military decision: Even though it was against the Jewish law to fight on the Sabbath, the Jews decided that they would defend themselves if attacked. They wouldn't initiate an attack, but they would not be passive under attack, either. Also, before Mattathias died, he appointed his successors—his second son, Simon, and his third son, Judah. He chose Simon because he felt Simon had good judgment and, as he said, Simon "shall be a father to you." Mattathias also said,

"Judah Maccabee, strong and mighty from his youth, will be your captain and will fight the battle of the people." Maccabee was Judah's nickname. Maccabee means "hammer," and in battle after battle, Judah dealt "hammer blows" to the Syrian army. The name stuck to describe all five brothers.

THE LEADERSHIP OF JUDAH

It's been estimated that Judah had 3,000 soldiers under his command. The Syrian army was more than ten times that size.

Not only was Judah's army outnumbered by the Syrians, it was outweaponed as well. Antiochus' army had the latest arms: ballistas which threw large stones, rams that battered the walls of the cities, bows and arrows, javelins, spears, and armor. They had foot soldiers, cavalry, and warrior elephants. The Jews had only farm animals and farm tools, which they converted into crude weapons. They used sticks and stones and whatever arms they were able to capture. It was like David fighting Goliath.

Judah was a brilliant fighter and an inspiring leader. He never lost sight of the Jewish goal—to regain control of the Temple of Jerusalem. Through centuries of foreign rule, the Temple had symbolized the right of the Jews to worship freely by the Laws of the Torah. This freedom was so essential to Jews that they continually risked their lives to fight for it.

Judah encouraged his men against great odds saying, "Victory in battle does not depend on the size of an army, but strength is from heaven. We are fighting for our lives and our laws. And He Himself will shatter them before us; but as for you, be not afraid of them."

The Maccabees' men trained well to fight. They knew the hills better than the Syrians did, but they didn't all hide in the mountains waiting for a chance to attack. That wasn't really possible since there was no way to feed so many soldiers. For much of the time the fighters stayed in their villages, farming or doing whatever they normally did. When it was time to wage a battle, they'd be sent for by a local leader.

It was a good system. While the soldiers were in their villages, they could keep their eyes and ears tuned for helpful information. The basic tactic of Judah's force was to attack and then retreat, jabbing constantly at the opposing troops. As more and more fighters joined the cause, the attacks became more harassing to Antiochus' forces, and Antiochus got more aggressive in his campaign.

FOUR MAJOR BATTLES

Four large battles were waged before the Jews regained control of the Temple. The first of these battles took place when a large army commanded by General Appolonius marched into the territory where Judah and his men were organized. Judah's force ambushed them, killing many of the soldiers and forcing the rest to flee. The Jews collected many weapons and a great deal of armor from that skirmish. Judah himself had killed General Appolonius and he kept the general's sword. Judah used that sword in battle for the rest of his life.

Another general, General Seron, heard about Appolonius' defeat. He decided to avenge this loss. His army was twice the size of Appolonius' army. He marched his army along the coast, heading south toward Jerusalem. They turned inland finally, and, in a pass in the mountains were attacked by Judah and his men who had been carefully watching their approach. Judah's men killed over 800 soldiers; the rest fled.

As news of the Maccabees' successes spread, more and more people joined the cause. Antiochus was furious. He was on his way to Persia to collect some tribute money, but before he left, he assigned half his army and elephants to the man he trusted most in the world, Lysias. Antiochus told Lysias, "Destroy the strength of Israel and the remnant of Jerusalem."

Lysias planned to do so. He chose his highest ranking generals to head the battle campaign. Altogether there were about 20,000 foot soldiers and cavalry. They didn't make the mistake of being ambushed in the mountains. They stuck to the plains where they could maneuver in the formations they were trained for. Besides, they knew that Judah's forces were more practiced at fighting in the hill country. They felt sure they would win. So were the slave dealers who came along in hopes of buying the defeated Jews, to sell later for a profit.

Judah and his men saw the army make their camp on the plains. They were struck with fear at the odds against them. But Judah was a persuasive leader who was able to instill great pride in his troops. "It is better for us to die in battle," he told them, "than to look upon the evils that have come upon our nation and our sanctuary."

The plan of the Syrian generals was to split their army and send half the soldiers to wage a surprise attack in the night on Judah's sleeping troops. The famous General Gorgias was to lead the attack. When the Maccabees' effective spy system learned of this plan, Judah had his men desert their camp. But they left fires burning as if they were really still there and asleep. Then Judah led his forces down to where the other half of the Syrian army was waiting and, before dawn, they attacked those sleeping soldiers. They were successful.

Meanwhile, Gorgias and his men had found the empty Jewish camp. He thought that Judah and his men were fleeing in retreat. He returned to his own camp, feeling triumphant. When Gorgias found a ruin of a campsite and all his dead soldiers, he realized that he had been outwitted.

The defeated survivors returned to Lysias. Lysias decided that he had to take care of this situation himself. He would lead the next attack on the Jews. He planned carefully, organizing 20,000 foot soldiers and over 3,000 cavalry. He took the same route as the other army, but he didn't want to fall into the same battle pattern. So he continued further on that route into more hilly country. This was more than Judah could have hoped for. He and his men were so well trained to fight in the hills that even though there were so many fewer Jews, they slaughtered 5,000 of Lysias' soldiers and caused many others to desert and flee.

Lysias was surprised at the intensity and determination in the way the Jews fought. He ordered a retreat and planned to go and enlist more soldiers for his army.

THE RECAPTURE OF THE TEMPLE

After this battle, even though the Jews knew that Lysias would attack again, they also knew they had won a major victory. They felt strong enough to march into Jerusalem and seize the Temple. The symbol of Jewish freedom had been held by the Syrians for three long years, and it had been in the hands of the hellenizers for many more.

Some of Judah's troops went ahead and fought off the enemy soldiers who were stationed at the Temple. When the rest of the troops arrived, they were horrified by what they saw. Their once beautiful Temple was in shambles. The gates of the Temple were charred from fire. Weeds grew in the courtyard. The altar was broken. The sanctuary was bare. Statues of Greek idols were everywhere.

People were so stunned and saddened that they fell to their faces on the ground. Many wept. And then they got to work to purify the Temple. They built a new altar from whole stones. They rebuilt the sanctuary and the inner parts of the Temple. They made new holy vessels and candlesticks. They baked breads and placed the loaves on the table. They hung new curtains.

Finally, early in the morning on the twenty-fifth day of the month of Kislev, the Jews began the celebration of the rededication of the Temple. People sang and chanted, accompanied by harps and lutes and cymbals. The front of the Temple was decked with gold crowns and small shields. Judah lighted the lamps of the Temple menorah. There was not very much oil to be had—only enough, it seemed, to burn for one day. But, according to legend, the oil lasted for eight days and the holy lamp stayed lighted for the entire celebration. Jews felt a great sense of joy and deep pride for their accomplishment. It was decreed at that time that Jews would observe this celebration every year for eight days to commemorate the rededication of the Temple.

THE STRUGGLE CONTINUED

The Temple was purified and the Jews celebrated, but still the fighting went on. Even though Antiochus died the year after the recapture of the Temple, the Syrians kept on sending armies into Judea. It wasn't enough for Judah and the other Maccabees to have regained the Temple. They wanted religious freedom established officially. That took more years of military battles. When religious freedom was granted, most of the Hasideans dropped out of the fighting.

But religious freedom wasn't enough for the Maccabees. They wanted total independence, all enemy troops out of Jerusalem, and no foreign rule of their land. Fighting for this took almost twenty more years and was finally achieved by Simon's negotiations. The only surviving Maccabee, Simon became the High Priest of Jerusalem and ruler of Judea. As Mattathias' second son, he began the rule of the Hasmoneans over the kingdom of the Jews in the year 143 B.C.E.

This was twenty-five years after the confrontation in the small village of Modi'in when Mattathias refused to accept the laws of the Syrian king, Antiochus. This was twenty-five years spent gathering troops, training them, hiding in the hills, attacking and retreating—always fighting against better-equipped armies with many more soldiers. This was twenty-five years of courageous and determined struggle for the right of Jews to live their lives as Jews, freely and openly, governed only by the Laws of the Torah. No wonder Hanukkah is a holiday that's been celebrated by Jews all over the world for more than 2,000 years.

THE CELEBRATION
OF CANDLES

When Judah and his followers rededicated the Temple, they found a tiny amount of oil. It seemed just enough to keep the Temple lamp lit for one day. But, according to legend, once the menorah was lit, it burned for eight days, all during the celebration.

Some say that this legend doesn't reveal the real meaning of Hanukkah, that it was the struggle of the Jews for religious freedom that's important to remember. It's true that the victory of the Maccabees is the main reason we celebrate Hanukkah. But lighting the candles has come to be the traditional way to celebrate the rededication of the Temple.

HOW TO LIGHT THE HANUKKAH CANDLES

Candles are lit each of the eight nights of Hanukkah. This is done using a menorah that is special for Hanukkah. In the Hanukkah menorah, there's one holder for each of the eight nights and one for the shammash. Shammash means servant in Hebrew; this is the candle that's used to light the others. Its holder should be in some way different from the others (higher or lower, for example).

The candle lighting is done in a traditional way. The candles to be lit on a night are placed in the menorah beginning from the right, and moving to the left starting with one candle (plus the shammash) and one more each day. New candles are used each night. The shammash gets lighted first, and then you use it to light the other candles, doing this from left to right. That means the newest candle is lit first each night. Then the shammash is put in its special holder.

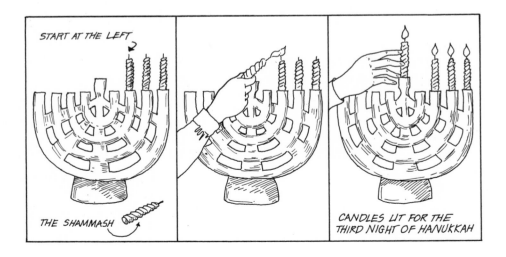

START AT THE LEFT

THE SHAMMASH

CANDLES LIT FOR THE THIRD NIGHT OF HANUKKAH

When the shammash is lighted, there are special prayers to say before the other candles are lit. Some people say these blessings in Hebrew. Some say them in English. Some say them both ways. These are the two blessings that are said every night:

Blessed are You, Lord our God, King of the Universe,
who has sanctified us with His commandments and
commanded us to kindle the Hanukkah lights.

בָּרוּךְ אַתָּה, יְיָ אֱלֹהֵינוּ, מֶלֶךְ הָעוֹלָם, אֲשֶׁר קִדְּשָׁנוּ
בְּמִצְוֹתָיו, וְצִוָּנוּ לְהַדְלִיק נֵר שֶׁל חֲנֻכָּה:

Ba-rooch a-ta a-do-nai, el-o-hey-nu me-lech ha-o-lam,
a-sher kid-shah-nu b'mitz-vo-tav, v'tzee-va-nu l'had-leek
ner, shel Ha-nuk-kah.

Blessed are You, Lord our God, King of the Universe,
who performed miracles for our ancestors in days gone
by, at this season of the year.

בָּרוּךְ אַתָּה, יְיָ אֱלֹהֵינוּ, מֶלֶךְ הָעוֹלָם, שֶׁעָשָׂה נִסִּים
לַאֲבוֹתֵינוּ, בַּיָּמִים הָהֵם, בַּזְּמַן הַזֶּה:

Ba-rooch a-ta a-do-nai, el-o-hey-nu me-lech ha-o-lam,
sheh-asa nee-seem la-a-vo-tey-nu ba-ya-meem ha-hem
baz-zman haz-zeh.

On the first of Hanukkah, one other blessing is also recited:

Blessed are You, Lord our God, King of the Universe,
who has granted us life and sustenance and permitted
us to reach this day.

בָּרוּךְ אַתָּה, יְיָ אֱלֹהֵינוּ, מֶלֶךְ הָעוֹלָם, שֶׁהֶחֱיָנוּ, וְקִיְּמָנוּ,
וְהִגִּיעָנוּ לַזְּמַן הַזֶּה:

Ba-rooch a-ta a-do-nai, el-o-hey-nu me-lech ha-o-lam,
sheh-hech-heh-ya-nu ve-kee-ye-ma-nu veh-hee-ghee-a-nu
laz-zman haz-zeh.

While the candles are being lit (or after they have been lit and
the shammash has been placed in its proper holder), the
tradition includes reciting the following:

We kindle these lights on account of the miracles, wonders,
and deliverances which You performed for our fathers in
those days at this time, by means of your holy priests. These
lights are sacred throughout all the eight days of Hanukkah;
we are not permitted to make any use of them, but only to
look at them, in order to give thanks to Your great Name for
Your miracles, wonders, and deliverances.

It's also customary to sing songs. "Rock of Ages" (*Maoz Tzur*) is
a traditional one. So are "O Hanukkah" and "Who Can Retell?"
You'll find words and music for these songs at the end of this
chapter.

This candle-lighting ceremony is done after sunset each night of Hanukkah. Forty-four candles are needed for the entire eight-day celebration, and the candles should burn for at least half an hour.

Many years ago, people would have their Hanukkah lights in the streets, outside their home. Then the custom became to have the lights in some sort of lantern hanging in the doorway. Today, many place their lit menorahs in a window. Then anyone passing by can see that Hanukkah is celebrated in that household, and they can tell which night of the celebration it is. When Antiochus IV ruled that Jews were not allowed to practice their religious beliefs, a display like this would have been impossible. Today, placing the lit candles in a window is a way to acknowledge our freedom to follow a belief without danger.

WHO LIGHTS THE CANDLES?

There's a certain excitement about lighting the candles. Families have found different ways to share the lighting so everyone gets a turn. Some take turns on different nights. Some pass the shammash around so more get a turn on one night. Some families have more than one Hanukkah menorah, maybe enough so everyone lights his or her own.

"There are four of us who take turns—my mother, my father, my sister, and me. This year I got to go first and light them the first night. My sister decided she wanted to go fourth. That was so she could do it the last night and light all eight."

—SARA ROSEMAN

"My brother and I usually take turns lighting the candles just before we eat. My dad says a prayer. We watch the candles burn during dinner and talk about the story of Hanukkah and why we light the candles."

—EVE LARNER

"On the first night my father lights them. On the second night, my father and mother light them. Then my father, mother, and the oldest child do it. And so on."

—GARY HIRSCHHORN

"We take turns lighting the candles with the shammash. The way we work it is one child lights all the candles that are supposed to be lit the first day. The second day the second child does it, and then it keeps going. We take turns. Sometimes we fight over who lights them the last day."

—JAY, BOB, AND SHARON BLUMENFIELD

"Whoever wants to lights them. Most of our family have their own Hanukkah menorahs and we all do our own."

—SERINA AND MURRAY MOORE

"We all share lighting the candles. My father lights the shammash and we do the others. It's not so good on the first night because there's only one. The sixth night is the best because then everyone in the family gets to light one. After that it doesn't work out so evenly anymore."

—JOAN SINGER

MORE ABOUT CANDLES

There are special candles made for Hanukkah that many people buy. This box of forty-four candles isn't very expensive. They are thin candles, about the same thickness as a pencil, almost four inches long, and in a variety of colors. Most Hanukkah menorahs are made with holders to fit these candles.

Eve Larner and her family don't buy these candles; they make their own. "We invite a whole bunch of friends over and we take turns dipping in the wax until it's all done. Then we start again. It's lots of fun. We play games and have a really good time. We make lots of candles."

If you're interested in trying this, the following instructions tell you how. It helps to invite other people to come, as Eve and her family do—dipping candles is time-consuming! Also, it's not a project to do without help from a grown-up, so talk about this with your parents. Hot wax can be dangerous if it accidentally spills.

◆ DIPPED CANDLES ◆

You'll need:
- wax
- wicks
- a knife
- scissors
- a saucepan
- a tin can for holding the wax, a little taller than you want the candles to be (a soup can will work for 3½-inch candles)
- a stove or electric hot plate

These directions work for making candles that are 3½ inches long.

Steps

1. Put some wax into the can. Place the can in a saucepan that is filled part way with water.

The wax gets melted when you heat the water. As the wax in the can melts, add some more until the level of melted wax is just ½ inch from the top of the can.

2. Take a long piece of wicking, about a yard long, and dip it into the wax. Pull it out and stretch it straight while the wax hardens. Then cut this into 6-inch lengths for each candle. This gives you 6 wicks.

Repeat until you have enough wicks for all 44 candles.

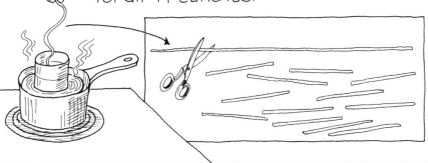

3. Now the dipping starts.

Dip a wick into the hot wax. Remove and let it harden. Dip again and remove. Repeat until the candle is as thick as you'd like it to be.

While you're doing this, **check the level of the wax** in the can, adding more to keep it the same as when you started. Otherwise, your candles will be fatter at the bottom.

4. Once a candle has been dipped, you need to shape it.

The bottom needs to be cut off with a heated knife. The candle needs to be straightened and rolled a bit on a smooth surface. The wick needs to be trimmed so it sticks up only ¼ inch above the candle.

- WICK DIPPED ONLY ONCE
- DIPPED ENOUGH TIMES, BUT SOFT AND SHAPELESS
- NOW IT'S BEEN STRAIGHTENED
- THE BOTTOM HAS BEEN CUT, AND THE WICK TRIMMED

Some hints:

▸ If the wax is too hot, it won't stick to the wicking so you'll have to lower the heat under the saucepan.

▸ Organize all the dippers so that you take turns dipping. That way, when yours is hardening, someone else can be dipping theirs.

▸ Give each person a square of cardboard to hold under the hardening candle so it doesn't drip all over the floor.

◆ ROLLED BEESWAX CANDLES ◆

Instead of dipping candles, you can make rolled ones. This is a way to avoid working with hot wax. You can buy sheets of beeswax for this in a variety of colors.

You'll need:
- sheets of beeswax
- wicks
- scissors

Steps

1. Cut a sheet of beeswax so it's about **3 or 4 inches** long. You can use a pair of scissors for this.

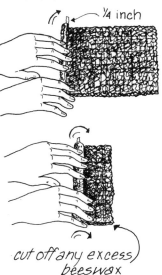

2. If the beeswax is very stiff, hold it near a heater for a few moments to soften it. Then place it on a flat surface.

¼ inch

3. Place a length of wick along one edge so it's even at one end, but sticks out about ¼ inch at the other. Fold the edge of the sheet over the wick to hold it evenly. Keep the fold straight.

4. Begin to roll. The trick is to **roll it tightly.** How thick you roll it depends on the size of the holder you'll be using.

cut off any excess beeswax

5. When you've finished rolling, press the edge of the beeswax so it sticks to the rest of the candle.

◆ OIL CANDLES ◆

When the Maccabees rededicated the Temple, they didn't use wax candles. They used oil in the Temple lamp. You can use oil at home for the Hanukkah lights by making your own oil candles. These are placed in a shallow bowl of water. Each night of Hanukkah, you add one more of your oil candles to the bowl. Use a candle and a separate candle holder for your shammash.

You'll need:
• a large shallow bowl, about 2 or 3 inches deep
• pipe cleaners for wicks — cut each in half
• aluminum foil, a 4-inch square for each candle
• oil — salad, cooking, or olive

Steps

1. Fold each square of foil in half and in half again so each is a 2-inch square.

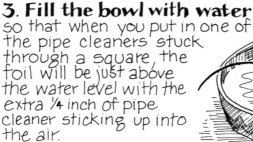

2. Push half a pipe cleaner through a small hole in the middle of each aluminum foil square. It should be sticking out of one side about ¼ inch. Coil the other end so it will stand up in a bowl.

3. Fill the bowl with water so that when you put in one of the pipe cleaners stuck through a square, the foil will be just above the water level with the extra ¼ inch of pipe cleaner sticking up into the air.

4. Gently pour some oil into the bowl until a **film of oil** covers the surface of the water. (Oil and water don't mix, and the oil floats on top.)

5. When you light the pipe cleaner, it will burn, using the oil for fuel! When the oil is used up, the water will put out the flame.

THE HANUKKAH MENORAH

Hanukkah menorahs have been made in many styles over the centuries. Some have been very simple, just providing the holders for the candles or for oil. Others have been very ornate, decorated in many different ways. Sometimes Judah Maccabee is shown. Sometimes they're decorated with sayings in Hebrew. Others use the Star of David. Elephants appear on some, representing the warrior elephants used by the Syrians. Hanukkah menorahs have been made of clay, brass, tin, wood, or lead, as well as from other materials. An American soldier who was fighting in the Korean War in the 1950s used brass shell casings to make a Hanukkah menorah; this one is part of the collection of the Jewish Museum in New York City.

You might want to make your own Hanukkah menorah, either for candles you make yourself, or for candles that you buy. There are lots of ways you can do this. Even if your family has a Hanukkah menorah, you might want to make another. That way, more of the family can have the chance to light candles during the celebration.

When making a menorah, there is no special shape or size it has to be. The candles can be in a straight line, or in a curve, or circle, or however you wish. There are no rules about the size of the candle holders, either. What is important is that the flames are kept separate in the menorah, so that they don't merge together into one larger flame. This separateness honors each night.

It's traditional on Hanukkah menorahs to have the candles for each of the eight nights at the same height, with only the shammash being higher. That's to show that no one night of Hanukkah is more important than any of the others. But many

Hanukkah menorahs are made with the candles in an up-and-down style.

Your Hanukkah menorah can be plain or fancy. It can be in one piece, or you can make a separate candle holder for each of the eight nights, and one more for the shammash. Using clay and shaping it into dreidels for the candle holders would work. You can make a menorah using materials you have in the house, like empty thread spools. If someone can help you use a drill, you might want to find a branch from a tree that has a shape you like, and drill holes in it for the candles. Use the drawings here to give you ideas, or invent your own design.

In the first century C.E. (Common Era), there was a debate among Jews about how the Hanukkah candles should be lit. Some felt that eight should be lit the first night, and one less each night after that, so that on the last night of Hanukkah, only one candle would burn. Others argued that increasing the candles each night was symbolic of increasing joy and light in this world. This feeling won out, and that is how Hanukkah candles are lit today. The kindling of the Hanukkah lights is one of the ways to honor the decree made by Judah Maccabee and his followers, that every year at the same time, the dedication of the Temple should be celebrated with gladness and joy for eight days.

◆ *Rock of Ages (Maoz Tzur)* ◆

Rock of Ag-es let our song

praise Thy sav-ing pow-er;

thou a-midst the ra-ging foes

wast our shelt'-ring tow-er

Fu-rious they as-sailed us,

but Thine arm a-vailed us

And thy word broke their sword

when our own strength failed us.

◆ O Hanukkah ◆

O Ha-nuk-ka, O Ha-nuk-ka, come light the me-no-rah!

Let's have a par-ty, we'll all dance the ho-rah. Gath-er

'round the ta-ble, we'll give you a treat, A drei-del to

play with, and lat-kes to eat. And while we are

play-ing The can-dles are burn-ing low. One for

each night, They shed a sweet light, To re-mind us

of days long a-go. One for each night, They shed

a sweet light, To re-mind us of days long a-go.

♦ *Who Can Retell?* ♦

Who can re-tell the things that be-fell us?

Who can count them?

In ev'ry age a he-ro or sage came to our aid.   Ah!

At this time of year in days of yore

Mac-ca-bees the Tem-ple did re-store

And to-day our peo-ple as we dreamed

will a-rise, u-nite, and be re-deemed.

WHEN DOES HANUKKAH COME THIS YEAR?

Sometimes Hanukkah comes very near the beginning of December; sometimes it comes later in the month. But it *always* comes on the twenty-fifth day of Kislev, and is celebrated through the second day of Tevet.

The calendar you generally use, that tells you when your birthday comes and when school lets out for summer vacation, isn't the same as the calendar that tells when Hanukkah starts. For that, you need to check a Jewish calendar. It works very differently from the regular Gregorian calendar. A bit of explaining may help you understand the difference.

Thousands of years ago, long before the time of the Maccabees, people realized that they needed some way to keep track of time. How else could they date religious holidays, or tell when they should plant their seeds? Try to imagine what life would be like today without a calendar. How would you keep track of birthdays and holidays? And would everyone keep track in the same way? It could be a terrible tangle.

People looked for clues to help solve the problem of measuring time. They didn't have to look too far. The sun was a totally reliable way to measure each day. Another clue was provided by the moon. People noticed that it changed from new moon to full moon and back to new moon again, in a repeating cycle that took about thirty days. The stars also provided some information. As time passes, certain groups of stars disappear over the horizon and other groups appear in their places. People noticed that this was tied to the different seasons. However, piecing these clues together to make a calendar wasn't such an easy job.

THE BABYLONIANS TURN TO THE MOON

The Babylonians decided that the moon was the most important timekeeper. They organized their calendar around it. Their calendar had twelve months, with each month being as long as one full cycle of the moon. This system hit a snag right away. Each month couldn't have the same number of days. That's because the cycle of the moon doesn't take exactly thirty days. It turns out that it takes just about twenty-nine and a half days for the moon to complete one cycle. And how can you make a calendar with a fraction of a day in it?

The Babylonians didn't worry about the fraction. They just made one month with 29 days, the next month with 30 days, the next with 29 days, and so on. By their system, the year had a total of 354 days. And that caused problems!

If you measure by the sun, a year is about 365 days long. That's roughly the amount of time it takes for the earth to make a complete trip around the sun, completing a cycle of the four seasons. The Babylonians' year was short by eleven days. So when they picked a month, that month came a little earlier the following year. And the next year, it came earlier still. By using just the moon, they ignored the fact that from one planting time to the next, the earth would have to make a complete trip around the sun. If they didn't pay some attention to the sun, their calendar would soon be telling them to go out and plant in the middle of winter.

They realized this would never do, and decided to fix the calendar. They started adding an extra month every three years or so to keep the calendar from going totally out of whack. There's a word that describes the process of adding extra days to a calendar to fix it—intercalation. Intercalation is done on leap years today, when an extra day is added to the end of February.

THE NINETEEN-YEAR CYCLE

After using their calendar system for about fifteen centuries, the Babylonians made another discovery. This one helped make their intercalations more accurate. They figured out a time connection between the sun and the moon. They learned that there is a way to have the solar year, as measured by the sun, and the lunar year, recorded by the twelve months of their calendar, come out even. It's a strange relationship that works on a nineteen-year cycle.

If you started to measure a year when the sun was at a certain starting position, and at that same time you started to measure a year by the lunar system of twelve cycles of the moon, you'd find that the lunar year takes fewer days than the solar year. But after nineteen solar years of time, both of the years will be ready to start again, at that same starting position, at the same time.

You might think of this idea this way. Suppose two friends came to visit you one Saturday, and the three of you had a fine time playing together. When one friend left, he said he'd be back to play every other day, coming again on Monday, then Wednesday, and so on. But your other friend said no, she couldn't come that often, that she would come every third day, and would be back on Tuesday, and then on Friday, and so on. According to the cycle of their visits, you could figure out when they'd both come again so all of you could spend another day together.

The Babylonian astronomers used this kind of figuring with the bigger problem of the sun and the moon. They discovered that the moon went through 12.37 cycles before the sun completed one cycle of a year, and that nineteen years according to the sun was almost exactly equal to 235 lunar months. Using this information, they were able to determine when to add extra months to their lunar calendar, to keep the seasons in order.

THE HANUKKAH CONNECTION

Now how does all this connect to Hanukkah? The Jewish calendar is modeled on the Babylonian system. It is based on both the moon and the sun.

According to the Jewish calendar, each New Year starts on the first day of the month of Tishri. That's the day nearest to the autumnal equinox, when the new moon appears. It falls in September or early October, according to our regular calendar.

The calendar has twelve basic months: Tishri, Heshvan, Kislev, Tevet, Shevat, Adar, Nisan, Iyyar, Sivan, Tammuz, Av, and Elul. The months are either 29 or 30 days long. To make the calendar work in rhythm with the length of the year as measured by the sun, a twenty-nine day month called Adar II is added seven times during every nineteen-year period. It's added in the third, sixth, eighth, eleventh, fourteenth, seventeenth, and nineteenth years of the cycle. This system works.

The Jewish calendar has one time measure that the Babylonians never included—the week. According to the Book of Genesis, the seventh day has special importance as the day of rest. Organizing days into seven-day weeks was started by the

Jews. The seventh day of the week is the only day that has a special name—Shabbat. The others are the first day, the second, and so on.

It was on the twenty-fifth day of the month of Kislev that the Jews began the celebration for rededicating the Temple after the Maccabean victory. And since that time each year, the Jewish calendar has to be consulted to see when Hanukkah starts.

Gregorian calendar
Jewish calendar

CALENDAR FOR PART OF
1982

Greg.	Jewish	Greg.	Jewish	Greg.	Jewish	Greg.	Jewish	Hanukkah
Oct. 19	2 Heshvan	5	19	22	6	9	23	
20	3	6	20	23	7	10	24	
21	4	7	21	24	8	11	25 HANUKKAH	1
22	5	8	22	25	9	12	26	2
23	6	9	23	26	10	13	27	3
24	7	10	24	27	11	14	28	4
25	8	11	25	28	12	15	29	5
26	9	12	26	29	13	16	30	6
27	10	13	27	30	14	17	1 Tevet	7
28	11	14	28	Dec. 1	15	18	2	8
29	12	15	29	2	16	19	3	
30	13	16	30	3	17	20	4	
31	14	17	1 kislev	4	18	21	5	
Nov. 1	15	18	2	5	19	22	6	
2	16	19	3	6	20	23	7	
3	17	20	4	7	21	24	8	
4	18	21	5	8	22	25	9	

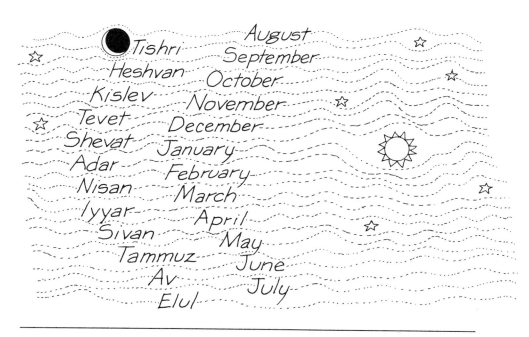

Tishri	August
Heshvan	September
Kislev	October
Tevet	November
Shevat	December
Adar	January
Nisan	February
Iyyar	March
Sivan	April
Tammuz	May
Av	June
Elul	July

THE GREGORIAN CALENDAR

The calendar that you usually use is called the Gregorian calendar. Most people in the world today, Jews included, use the Gregorian calendar on a daily basis. It seems necessary to have one calendar for world use so people can communicate with each other sensibly.

The Gregorian calendar doesn't pay much attention to the moon at all; it is strictly based on the solar year. The years on the Gregorian calendar are numbered differently than on the Jewish calendar. The first Jewish calendar year corresponds to the year 3761 B.C. of the Gregorian calendar.

On many Gregorian calendars, Jewish holidays are noted, just as are national holidays and Christian holidays. Just the first day is usually marked for Hanukkah; so you can tell when it starts. But it's a little confusing even so. You begin lighting the candles for Hanukkah on the night before the first day.

According to the Jewish way of tracking time, days really begin the evening before they're noted on the calendar. This stems from the creation of heaven and earth as told in the very first book of the Bible, Genesis. The first chapter of Genesis tells about God creating light and dividing it from darkness, and calling these divisions of time day and night. When we say day, we include both day and night and usually think of the day as coming first. According to Jewish tradition, however, it's the other way around. The Sabbath, the day of rest, begins after the work of the sixth day of the week has been completed, with the onset of twilight. Similarly, for Hanukkah, candles are lit soon after sunset preceding each of the eight days of the celebration.

WHY THE MOON AND NOT THE SUN?

Jews continue to use the Jewish calendar to set all religious holidays, paying attention to the phases of the moon. In each cycle, the new moon appears, grows to a full moon, and then gets smaller and finally disappears. The disappearance of the moon is like a death, but this death is always followed by rebirth, when the new moon appears. Organizing the calendar by the cycles of the moon is one way to pay special honor to this cycle which seems to many like our basic life cycle. During Hanukkah the moon is in the same phase of its cycle each year, with the new moon appearing on the sixth night.

Even though the moon gets first importance in the calendar, the sun can't be ignored as a marker of time. After all, without the sun there would be no life.

The complicated system of intercalation of nineteen-year cycles enables the Jewish calendar to keep in step with the seasons of the year. And so Hanukkah comes at a time when the celebration of lights helps brighten long winter nights.

A TIME TO EAT

Food helps to make any celebration more special. That's because eating is a festive way for people to share important times together. It helps make occasions truly memorable.

It's traditional to eat certain foods at Hanukkah. These special dishes do more than make a Hanukkah feast delicious. They serve as reminders of the holiday—a way to honor the story of the struggle even while you're having a good time eating.

POTATO LATKES

Latke is the Yiddish word for pancake. Potato latkes are one of the most popular Hanukkah foods. They're made from grated potatoes and grated or chopped onions that are held together with eggs and some flour and cooked by being fried in oil.

Since the oil was an important part of the rededication of the Temple after the struggle of the Maccabees, eating foods cooked in oil has become one way to symbolize the victory.

But the custom of latkes did not start in the time of the Maccabees. It couldn't have. The Maccabees had never even heard of potatoes. Though potatoes grew wild in South America, they never left that part of the world until the Spanish explorer Pizarro brought them to Europe in the 1500s. That was centuries after the struggle that led to the celebration of Hanukkah! Once potatoes were cultivated in Europe, they became a common and plentiful food for people. Jews living in Eastern Europe started to make potato latkes in the 1600s, using this common food in a special way that made it more festive.

There is no one way to make potato latkes; every cook has his or her own secret. But one thing is certain: Making potato latkes is a job that's more fun if people do it together. Peeling and grating potatoes is a large chore and it's easier if several people help. Frying the latkes can't be done all at once. People's appetites are usually bigger than the number of latkes a frying pan can hold. Besides, helping to make latkes can be one more way to celebrate Hanukkah. Check with the chief cook in your family, and volunteer.

In many families, there's a favorite recipe that someone has learned from someone else. This may be true in your family. If not, here's one that works to make some very tasty latkes. This recipe will make about fifteen latkes.

◆ POTATO LATKES ◆

Ingredients

- 5 medium-sized potatoes
- 1 small onion
- ½ to 1 teaspoon salt
- ¼ teaspoon pepper
- 2 tablespoons flour
- 2 eggs
- salad oil

Steps

1. Peel the potatoes.

If you're not going to use them right away, put them in a bowl and cover them with cold water.

2. Grate the potatoes into a bowl.

It really doesn't matter which holes of the grater you use. Larger holes are the only ones that will do the job, some people think, since they produce crunchier latkes. Others insist on using the medium-sized holes for smoother latkes. It's up to you. But one thing everyone agrees on. *Watch your knuckles,* especially when you're near the end of a potato. Grated knuckles can hurt.

3. Grate the onion into the same bowl.

(Peel the skin off first.)

4. Get rid of the liquid

that has collected in the bowl. Either pour it out carefully, or put the mixture in a sieve and press out the extra liquid.

(clean hands!)

5. Beat the eggs in another bowl and then **add to the potato/onion mixture.**

6. Add the flour, salt, and pepper. Mix well.

1 Tbsp.

SALT ½ tsp.

Pepper ¼ tsp.

FLOUR

1 Tbsp.

7. Turn the oven to 250°.
This is so you can keep the first latkes you fry warm while you're cooking the rest.

8. Pour enough **salad oil** into the bottom of a large frying pan so it's about ¼ inch deep. **Heat the oil,** and keep it hot at medium to medium high heat. **Put a tablespoon** of the **batter** into the oil and **press it with a slotted pancake turner** to a thin pancake. Do as many of these as the pan will hold. **Each latke gets turned once.**

You can tell when they're ready to turn because the edges get brown. You should cook the latkes so they're golden brown and crisp on each side. As they're done, put them in a shallow pan lined with some paper towels and keep them warm in the oven.

SOME EXTRA HINTS: As you're frying the latkes, check the oil level and add more if you need to keep it up to ¼ inch deep. When you add extra oil, let it heat up before you add more batter. Also, as the extra batter is sitting and waiting to be cooked into latkes, liquid will collect at the bottom. Don't bother pouring this off; just stir the batter from time to time.

ALONG WITH THE LATKES

Latkes are usually eaten with sour cream and applesauce. Making applesauce isn't hard. You might want to make some yourself ahead of time for the Hanukkah meal, but check with your parents first.

◆ APPLESAUCE ◆

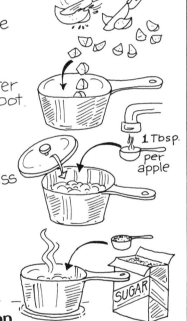

Ingredients
- apples, at least one per person
- sugar
- ground cinnamon

Steps

1. Peel the apples. Cut them into quarters and cut out the seeds and core. Then cut each quarter into 3 smaller pieces. Put all the pieces into a saucepan.

2. Add water to the saucepan, measuring 1 tablespoon of water for each apple you put into the pot.

3. Cover and cook over **low heat** until the apples are soft enough to mash. This will take 15 to 20 minutes. Test for softness with a fork.

1 Tbsp. per apple

4. Add 1 tablespoon of **sugar** for each apple you used. Stir this into the apples. Cover and cook for 3 minutes more.

5. Mash with a potato masher or fork. Sprinkle with **cinnamon**.

This applesauce is good to eat warm or cold.

HANUKKAH DESSERTS

Some people use the oil that symbolizes Hanukkah to cook sweet desserts. In Israel, fried doughnuts filled with jelly are popular; they're called sufganiyot. Sometimes the desserts are pastry puffs dipped in honey or covered with powdered sugar. Some are snail-shaped sweets. They are all deep fried in oil, using much more oil than is used for latkes. During the time of the Maccabees, people did eat sweet pastries that were fried, and some families today like to have such a dessert to remind them of the Maccabean victory.

Making fried pastries can be complicated. But if you have a sweet tooth and want to help prepare a dessert that's good to eat and also helps to celebrate Hanukkah, try making cookies in special Hanukkah shapes. To do this, you need some cookie dough that can be rolled out and then cut into shapes you've designed. Gingerbread cookies work for this; so do sugar cookies. The recipe here will work. You may want to get some help from your parents in preparing the dough if you're not too practiced in the kitchen.

Leave yourself enough time for this recipe. It has to chill for three hours before you roll it out to cut. Make the dough early in the day. Then while it's chilling, you'll have plenty of time to draw your designs on paper and cut them out. Use your cut-outs right on the rolled dough, cutting around them with a knife.

SOME COOKIE SHAPES TO TRY....

HANUKKAH CANDLE

STAR OF DAVID

SYRIAN WAR ELEPHANT

◆ SUGAR COOKIES ◆

Ingredients
- ½ cup sugar (white or brown)
- ½ cup butter (at room temperature so it's soft)
- 2 eggs
- 2½ cups all purpose flour
- 2 teaspoons double-acting baking powder
- 1 teaspoon vanilla

Steps

1. When the **butter** is at room temperature, **cream it with sugar.** Do this with an electric mixer, or by using the back of a wooden spoon, mushing the sugar into the butter against the side of the mixing bowl.

2. Beat in all the rest of the ingredients.

1 tsp. VANILLA • BAKING POWDER • 2 tsp. • 2 eggs • FLOUR • 2½ C.

3. Cover the bowl and put it in the **refrigerator** for **3 to 4 hours.** If you skip this step, it will be quite a mess to roll and cut the cookies. You'll have to use extra flour to keep it from being too sticky, and then your cookies will not taste terrific. So be patient.

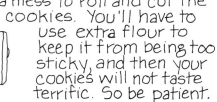

4. When you're ready to roll out the dough, **use a rolling pin** and **roll the dough** until it's **very thin**, about as thin as a nickel. Use a little flour on the rolling pin and on the surface you're rolling it out on, but as little as possible. **Cut the shapes out with a small knife**, like a paring knife.

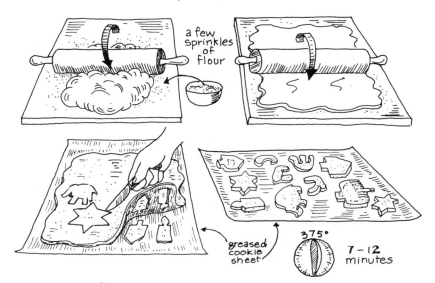

a few sprinkles of flour

greased cookie sheet

375°

7–12 minutes

5. Preheat the oven to 375°. Grease a cookie sheet and **bake** your creations for 7 to 12 minutes. That means after 7 minutes, take a peek. The time it takes to cook them depends on how thin you rolled the dough.

Use the shapes shown for starter ideas. Invent your own designs also. When the cookies are done, serve them to your family. It might be fun to have everyone tell how they think the cookies you made are connected to Hanukkah. Then they can compare their explanations with what you thought when you made them.

A HINT FOR YOUR COOKIES: Place the rolled dough on a greased cookie sheet first. Then cut out your shapes and you can lift off the extra. The less you handle the dough, the better your cookies will turn out. Don't waste the extra, though. Make it into a ball and then roll it out to make more cookies.

Use a fork prong to draw on the dough

A HANUKKAH MENORAH

A DREIDEL

SHIN

GIMMEL

HEH

NUN

OTHER HANUKKAH FOODS

There are other foods that some families have traditionally eaten during Hanukkah. One is roast goose for the main course. That custom came from Eastern Europe many, many years ago, when geese were best to eat during the winter. People raised their own, and besides having a good meal from them, there was a lot more of the goose to use or sell—the feathers for quills, the down for pillows, the fat for cooking, the neck for stuffing, the liver for pâté. In Germany in the 1500s, geese were called "the Jew's fowl, " since they were so widely used.

Sauerbraten is the main course of a Hanukkah feast for many. It's a pot roast made from a chunk of beef that's been marinated before it's cooked.

In Spain, some Jews have a special celebration on the sixth night of Hanukkah. That's always the night of the new moon, and the special dinner that's served then includes a dish called couscous. It's a dish made with bulgur wheat and ground lamb, with onions, celery, honey, and raisins.

WHAT MAKES SPECIAL FOODS SO SPECIAL?

Fixing these foods for Hanukkah helps to make that occasion unique, different from all the other meals of the year. It's a tradition that helps you to think about what is so special about this time. It's a way of saying: Hanukkah is important.

What's not important is whether you eat sour cream or yoghurt or sugar with your latkes, or really whether you eat latkes at all. Latkes are part of a tradition that's been carried on for over three hundred years to honor the Maccabean victory. The Maccabees themselves never even ate them. But still the preparing of a special dish and the eating together is a way to recall what struggle and courage can do, and how the idea of religious freedom was so important to some people that they risked their lives to fight for it—and won. What better way to honor that victory than to have a joyous celebration! And what's a celebration without delicious food!

A TIME TO PLAY

Dreidel is the most popular game played during Hanukkah. It's a gambling game. It seems that gambling games have long been a tradition for the evenings during the celebration of Hanukkah. Some say the game was used long ago when Jewish people were forbidden to come together and pray. So they'd pretend they were playing with the little top when they were really praying. Others say that dreidel was played just because it's fun, and Hanukkah is a time for fun.

The game works for two players or for a mob. Anyone can play, from little kids to grown-ups. That's because no special skill is needed—just a bit of a gambling streak. What you need to get a game started are a dreidel and ten or fifteen objects for each player. Some people play for pennies. Some play for dried beans or toothpicks. Some prefer to use some sort of munchies, like sunflower seeds, raisins, or popcorn. Use whatever you've got around the house. If you use any of the munchies to play with, give each player his or her own pile, and then make sure to have another bowl around for snacking. Playing dreidel has been known to make people crave something to chew on when the game gets exciting.

THE DREIDEL

The dreidel used today is like the top used in Germany many, many years ago with the letters changed to Hebrew letters: נ (nun), ג (gimmel), ה (heh), שׁ (shin). Each letter stands for the first letter in the four words of the Hebrew message: נֵס גָּדוֹל הָיָה שָׁם (*nais gadol hayah sham*). It means "A great miracle happened there." The miracle occurred when the Maccabees recaptured the Temple of Jerusalem.

In modern Israel today, they've changed the "there" to "here," so instead of the letter ‎ש‎ (shin), the initial of *sham* (there), the dreidel uses ‎פ‎ (pe), the initial of *poh* (here). Some people use dreidels that have the letters N, G, H, and S on them, instead of the Hebrew letters.

You can find dreidels in many shapes and sizes. Fancy ones have been made of lead, molded from clay, or carved in wood. Even more elaborate dreidels have been made of silver or ivory. Plastic ones work well and are inexpensive to buy. You can also make your own, using cardboard for simpler versions or wood for a more difficult project. Try making a dreidel from one of the three different ways shown. You can make one for yourself, or as a Hanukkah gift for someone else. If you give a dreidel for a gift, it's helpful to include the rules for playing the game—they're hard for some people to remember from year to year.

◆ HOW TO PLAY DREIDEL ◆

Make sure that everyone who is playing starts with the same number of objects.
You only need one dreidel since everyone takes turns spinning it.
Also, make sure you all agree on the rules before the gambling gets going.

1. Each player puts one from his or her pile of objects into the center, called the pot.

2. A player spins the dreidel; the letter that comes up tells what to do:

נ (nun) : *The player does nothing; the next player spins.*

ג (gimmel) : *The player takes all that's in the pot; everyone puts one more in before the next person spins.*

ה (heh) : *The player takes half of what's in the pot (or half plus one extra if there's an odd number in the pot).*

ש (shin) : *The player puts one into the pot.*

3. Whenever the pot is empty, or there's only one left in it, every player has to put one in before the next spin.

4. The game is over when one player has won everything, and everyone else is wiped out.

There really aren't any official dreidel rules. Some people play with slightly different variations. For example, some say that if ש (shin) comes up, you have to pay two into the pot instead of one. Some play until just one player loses all he or she started with, and the winner is the person who has the most at that time. Some play that players put one into the pot before each spin, whether or not the pot is down to one or empty.

The Yiddish variation is slightly different. Yiddish uses Hebrew letters so that נ (nun) stands for the Yiddish word *nem* which means take. Gimmel stands for *gunesh*, which means nothing. Heh stands for *half*, which means half. Shin stands for *shtel*, which means put into (the pot). In this version of the game the meaning of nun and gimmel are reversed.

MAKING YOUR OWN DREIDEL

◆ #1. A QUICK AND EASY DREIDEL ◆

You'll need these materials:
- heavy cardboard, such as the top of a supermarket carton or the back piece of a pad of paper
- scissors
- a ruler
- colored markers or crayons
- a short stub of a pencil, about 3 inches long

Steps:

1. Cut a square from the cardboard. If it's very heavy, you may need some help doing this. Make the square about **2 to 3 inches on a side.**

2. Draw lines from corner to corner. This divides the square into four sections and also marks the center of it.

3. Draw the symbols in each section as shown.

4. Poke a hole through the center carefully with the point of the scissors. Then insert the pencil, twisting it to work it down. The pencil should stick out the bottom as far as it needs to spin easily, usually a little more than an inch. Experiment to find where it spins best.

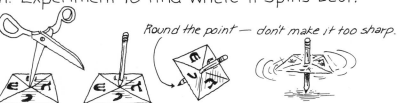

Round the point — don't make it too sharp.

◆ #2. THE CARDBOARD CUBE DREIDEL ◆

You'll need these materials:
• cardboard from a shirt cardboard, large index card, or a file folder; a cardboard carton is too heavy
• scissors
• a ruler
• glue
• colored markers or crayons
• a short stub of a pencil, about 4 inches long
• tracing paper or other paper light enough to trace through

Steps:

1. **Cut a pattern**, as shown on the next page from the cardboard. Do this by tracing the pattern onto tracing paper or other thin paper.

Then turn your tracing over and rub over the back of the outline of the pattern with the side of a pencil lead. Turn the paper back and put it on top of the cardboard you're going to use. Draw over the outline of the shape, pressing hard with your pencil. When you lift up the tracing paper, the outline will be on the cardboard. Cut it out carefully.

color the letters

pattern for the
CARDBOARD CUBE DREIDEL

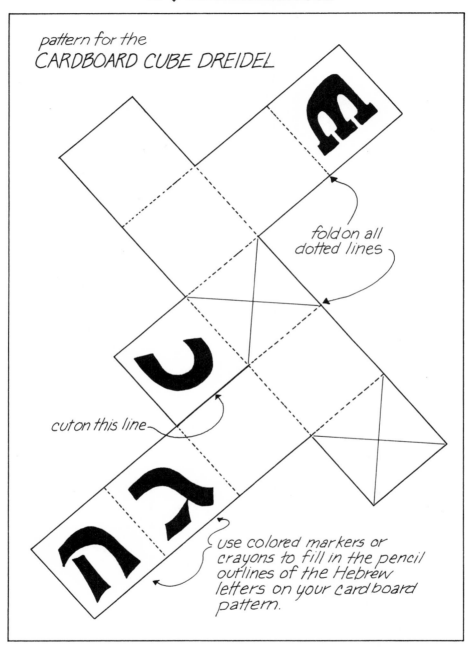

fold on all
dotted lines

cut on this line

use colored markers or
crayons to fill in the pencil
outlines of the Hebrew
letters on your cardboard
pattern.

2. Make a careful fold on each of the dotted lines.
If the cardboard is very stiff, it helps to score the lines first before folding. You do this by holding a ruler against the line and lightly running the point of the scissors down the line to make a slight indentation. It should fold more easily now.

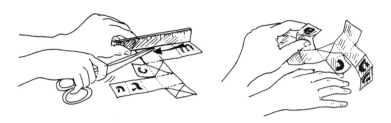

3. Fold the shape to make a cube.
Make sure to fold it so the Hebrew letters are showing, as well as the 2 squares with the lines drawn from corner to corner.

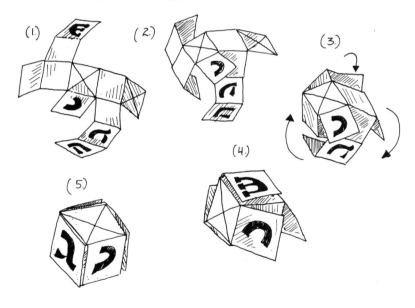

4. Use glue to hold the cube together.

You'll need to use glue on the back of each of the sides with the Hebrew letters, as well as on one of the squares with the X on it.

Let the glue dry before going on to step 5.

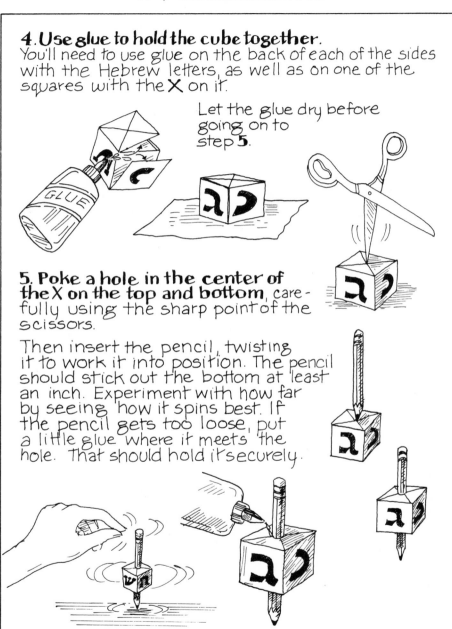

5. Poke a hole in the center of the X on the top and bottom, carefully using the sharp point of the scissors.

Then insert the pencil, twisting it to work it into position. The pencil should stick out the bottom at least an inch. Experiment with how far by seeing how it spins best. If the pencil gets too loose, put a little glue where it meets the hole. That should hold it securely.

◆ #3. A WOODEN DREIDEL ◆

You'll need some help from an adult who has some woodworking skills, since there's drilling and sawing to be done.

You'll need these materials:
- a cube of wood, at least 1 inch on a side, with a 5/16 inch hole drilled through the center of it
- a piece of dowel, 5/16 inch in diameter and 3 inches long
- a vise
- a wooden mallet or hammer
- a pencil sharpener
- sandpaper
- colored markers
- semigloss clear varnish or plastic coating (optional)

Steps:

1. Getting the cube with the hole drilled in it is the part where you'll need adult help. The hole has to be in the center for the dreidel to spin well. **Once you've got the cube, sand the sides.** Do this by placing the sandpaper flat on a workspace and rubbing the cube's faces on it until they're smooth.

2. Put a point on the dowel by using a pencil sharpener. Don't make it real pointy; a rounded tip is best. Use the sandpaper if you need to.

3. Use a vise to hold the cube firmly, hole up. Then **tap in the dowel** using a **wooden mallet or hammer.**

When you've hammered it down so about half an inch is sticking out of the bottom, try spinning it to **see how it spins.** You may want to tap it down a bit farther, but **hammer it just a bit at a time** and experiment.

4. Draw the Hebrew letters on the faces of the cube. Draw them in **pencil first**, and then carefully go over them with a **marking pen.**

5. If you wish, **protect your dreidel with a clear finish.** Before you do this, tap a small **nail or thumbtack** in the **top end of the dowel.**

Then **use a piece of wire or paper clip** to wind around so you can hang the dreidel while it's drying.

You can use a **jar** and a **small stick** across the top for this. Coat the dreidel, and then hang it as shown.

A DREIDEL SONG

It's not a good idea to make a dreidel from clay. It won't spin very well and it will be too breakable. But this song uses the word clay for the rhyme. (Maybe you can figure your own way to change the verse.) Each of the verses is sung to the same tune.

Oh, drei-del drei-del drei-del, I made it out of clay.

And when my drei-del's rea-dy, Oh, drei-del I will play.

1 Oh, dreidel, dreidel, dreidel,
  I made it out of clay.
  And when my dreidel's ready,
  Oh, dreidel I will play!

2 I'll take my little dreidel
  And give it a good strong spin.
  I hope it lands on Gimmel,
  For then I'm sure to win.

3 If I spin Heh, I take half,
  But none if I spin Nun.
  I get the pot with Gimmel
  With Shin I must pay one.

GIVING AND GETTING

Presents have long been a part of celebrating Hanukkah. Traditionally, presents were given mainly to children, and usually presents were Hanukkah gelt. Gelt means money, and for Hanukkah, the money given was most often coins.

This tradition is linked to the Jews finally winning their total independence. That was about twenty-five years after the rededication of the Temple under Judah's leadership. Simon had become the leader of the Jews at that time. Demetrius, the king who granted their independence, had a letter written to Simon: "I permit you to mint your own coinage as money for your country. Jerusalem and the Temple shall be free."

The right to make their own money was a privilege won as a result of the long struggle. It was the legal recognition of true independence. And because of this, some people today still give money during Hanukkah as a way to remember the victory. There are also candy coins which are popular to give, chocolate ones wrapped in gold foil paper. It's a way to honor the tradition of Hanukkah gelt that also tastes good.

Giving presents during Hanukkah has expanded beyond just giving money to children. In some families, not only do the children receive presents, but they give presents as well, often to friends and relatives. This is another aspect of celebrating Hanukkah where the rituals that families follow differ from each other.

In the Blumenfield family, Jay, Bob, and Sharon get presents each night of Hanukkah. Their parents hide a present for each of them every night, and they get to search the house for them. Mostly they get little presents except on the last night, when they each get a big one. They also get gifts from their grandparents and give presents to their parents and to each other.

In the Singer family, the children get presents from their parents, their grandparents, and from each other. Joan writes that they get Hanukkah gelt as well as other presents, but all on the first night. At that time, she and her two sisters and her brother take turns opening what they have received. Joan uses her allowance for the presents she buys for her sisters, her brother, her parents, and her grandparents.

Jonathan Rosen usually gets just one big Hanukkah present from his parents. He also gets money from other relatives. Jonathan saves money to buy the Hanukkah gifts he gives to all the members of his family.

Elizabeth and Jason Burns also get money for Hanukkah from their relatives, and a present from their parents on each of the nights of Hanukkah. Liz writes that she either makes the presents she gives or buys them from money she's saved from her allowance.

Making presents is one solution to your Hanukkah gift-giving. Sometimes it's easy to know just what would be a perfect gift for a person, and sometimes it's really hard to think of something that feels right. When thinking about gifts for Hanukkah, it's possible to make presents that people will enjoy and that also have a connection to why Hanukkah is celebrated. A starter collection of gift ideas that you can make is included here. You may want to try some of these, or they may spark some ideas of your own.

A CANDLE BOX

Make a box that holds all forty-four candles for Hanukkah, and decorate it. Each of the boxes described looks nice when both the tops and the edges are decorated. On the tops, you may want to draw a Hanukkah menorah or a dreidel, and add a greeting. Along the edges, make a border of coins, or candles, or elephants, or some other design. Read through the directions for the two different boxes and see which you're more interested in making.

◆ CANDLE BOX NUMBER ONE ◆

This box is folded from **heavy paper**, such as construction drawing paper. The heavier the paper, the sturdier the box. **To make a box with a lid** that holds the traditional size Hanukkah candles, you need **two squares** of the paper you choose, **one** that measures **11 inches on a side** and **one** that measures **11¼ inches on a side**. The larger piece is for the lid.

The directions are the same for folding each piece. Make the bottom of the box first with the 11-inch square. The top will be more visible when you're done, and so, if you need practice, you might as well get it on the bottom of the box.

Before you fold the top totally, add your decorations. Do this by following the directions up to the step where you have to make the four cuts. Then use the fold lines as guides to see where to decorate the top of the lid, as well as the sides.

Steps:

1. Crease the square along each of the dotted lines as shown.
2. Fold one corner up to meet the center of the square.

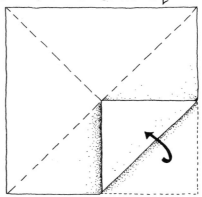

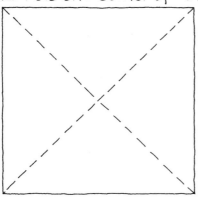

3. Then fold that folded edge up to the center point again.
Be careful not to let the original corner slip out past the center point when you fold the edge up.

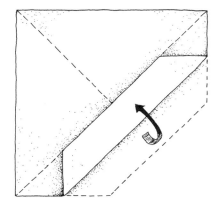

4 Unfold this and do the same with each of the other corners.

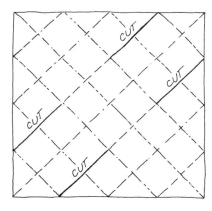

When you get finished, your square will have folds on all the dotted lines in the drawing.

★ *Decorate the box top at this point.*

Cut along the four folds exactly as shown.

5. Fold in two opposite corners on the first fold line.

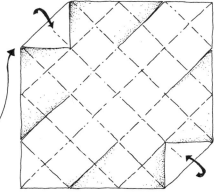

6. Fold in each of those edges.

7. Then fold up each of the four flaps as shown.

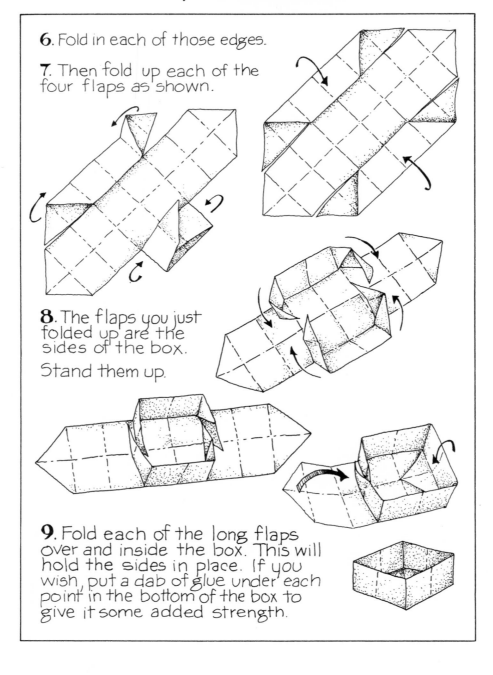

8. The flaps you just folded up are the sides of the box.

Stand them up.

9. Fold each of the long flaps over and inside the box. This will hold the sides in place. If you wish, put a dab of glue under each point in the bottom of the box to give it some added strength.

◆ CANDLE BOX NUMBER TWO ◆

This box can be made from **cardboard or tagboard**. It's made all in one piece. Manila file folders work well; you can make two of these boxes from one folder. This box will also hold all forty-four of the regular Hanukkah candles.

Steps:

1. First you need to draw the pattern shown onto the cardboard or tagboard you're using for the box. Use a ruler to draw the lines as straight as possible, and measure carefully. It may be easiest to rule all the squares as shown, making them each half an inch on a side. Then the pattern is clear to outline.

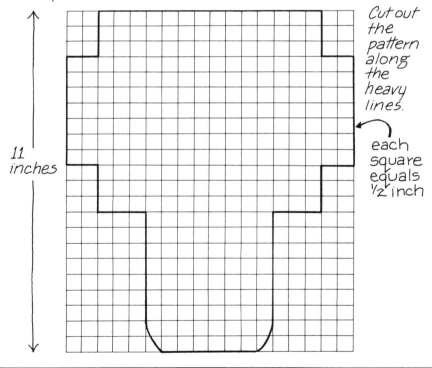

11 inches

Cut out the pattern along the heavy lines.

each square equals ½ inch

2. With the side of the pencil lines facing up, score each of the lines shown. This will make it easier to fold the box. You score a line by placing a ruler along it and gently running the point of a pair of scissors down the line to make a slight indentation.

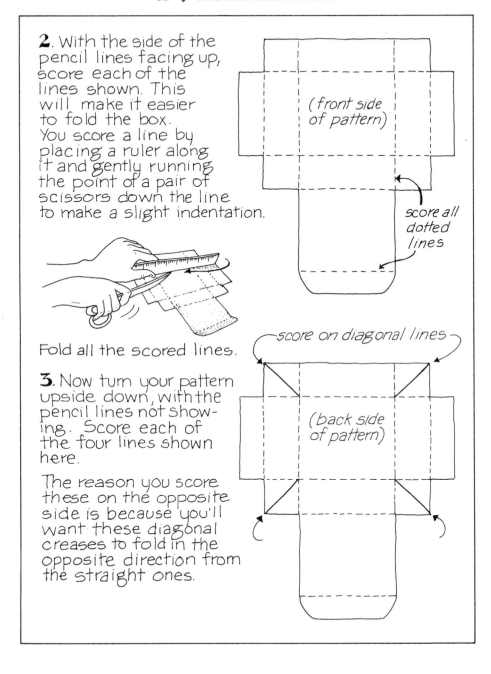

(front side of pattern)

score all dotted lines

Fold all the scored lines.

3. Now turn your pattern upside down, with the pencil lines not showing. Score each of the four lines shown here.

The reason you score these on the opposite side is because you'll want these diagonal creases to fold in the opposite direction from the straight ones.

score on diagonal lines

(back side of pattern)

4. This is the best time to decorate your box. Do this on the side with the pencil lines. You may want to erase the lines first.

Use the sample shown to see where the top and sides of the box will be once it's folded.

sides

top

5. Fold up the box. You'll need to use some glue or tape to hold it in shape. Fold the triangular pieces toward the short sides of the box.

GLUE

Add glue to the corners.

A DREIDEL PRESENT

Follow the directions suggested in Chapter 5 to make a dreidel for a Hanukkah present. Make a box for the dreidel using the directions for either of the candle boxes explained on pages 88–93. Write out the rules for playing dreidel in a little booklet that will fit into the box.

◆ STUFF A DREIDEL ◆

If you like to sew, you might want to make this toy for a younger brother or sister. This dreidel won't spin very well, but it's nice and squeezy. You don't need much material; check with your parents for remnants you can choose from.

You'll need these materials:
- scissors to cut the fabric
- needle
- thread
- marking pens to write the Hebrew letters
- shredded foam or other pillow stuffing to stuff it with

Steps:

1. Cut out three pieces of fabric using this pattern.

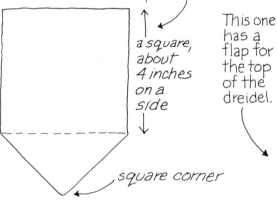

a square, about 4 inches on a side

square corner

2. Cut out a fourth piece using this pattern.

This one has a flap for the top of the dreidel.

3. Cut one piece of fabric from this pattern for the handle on the top.

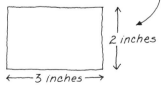

2 inches

← 3 inches →

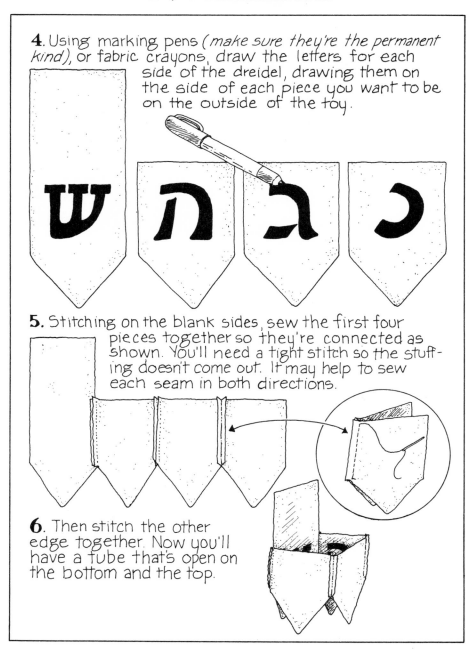

4. Using marking pens *(make sure they're the permanent kind),* or fabric crayons, draw the letters for each side of the dreidel, drawing them on the side of each piece you want to be on the outside of the toy.

5. Stitching on the blank sides, sew the first four pieces together so they're connected as shown. You'll need a tight stitch so the stuffing doesn't come out. It may help to sew each seam in both directions.

6. Then stitch the other edge together. Now you'll have a tube that's open on the bottom and the top.

7. Stitch the pointy end, sewing each edge to the edge next to it. This makes the tip of the dreidel.

8. Sew the top flap to two of the three remaining edges leaving the other one open for stuffing the dreidel.

leave open

9. Turn the fabric right side out. Stuff it until it's puffy and firm.

10. Stitch the remaining side closed.

11. For the handle, take the last piece of fabric and stitch it as shown on two sides.

12. Turn it right side out and stuff. Sew the open side, pulling the thread so it puckers and pulls that edge together.

13. Sew the handle to the middle of the top of the dreidel.

◆ A STAR FOR YOUR POCKET ◆

This project tells how to make a fold-up Star of David that opens up to lie flat as well.

You'll need these materials:
• thin cardboard or tagboard
• masking tape
• scissors

Steps:
1. Cut 24 triangles just like this one. Don't change the shape of them or you won't be able to make the six-pointed star!

2. Lay out a long strip of tape, sticky side up.

3. Place the triangles on the tape like this. Do this for all 24 triangles.

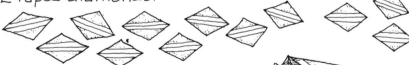

4. Cut the triangles apart into pairs so you have 12 taped diamonds.

5. Take two diamonds and tape them together as shown. Make sure to have an extra piece of tape hanging over.

6. Fold triangle **1** over onto triangle **2**. Then fold triangle **4** over onto triangle **3**. Press down firmly for the tape to stick. This gives you one point of the star.

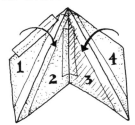
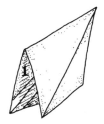

Follow steps **5** and **6** for all the triangles. You should have six points when you're done.

7. To assemble your star, fold each of the points like this.

Arrange them on a flat surface as shown and tape. Leave one side untaped.

Flip the star over and tape the other side, too.

Be careful to leave the same slit untaped on both sides!

FOLDED STAR

OPEN STAR

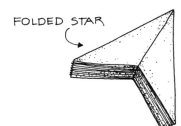
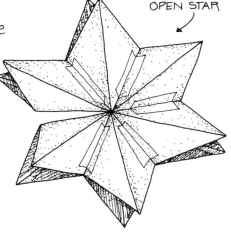

A PRESENT TO EAT

There's a recipe for making cookies on pages 65–67 along with suggestions for making the cookies into shapes that symbolize Hanukkah. You might want to make a batch as a present for someone you know who likes to munch on cookies. Include a card that explains the shapes and what they have to do with Hanukkah. Or, invent a little quiz for them to guess the shapes. They can check with you for the right answers.

MORE PRESENT POSSIBILITIES

These gift-making ideas are just starters for you. You may want to make your own Hanukkah greeting cards, or wrapping paper decorated with Hanukkah symbols. Maybe you'd like to be really ambitious and make a set of Hanukkah candles as a gift for someone. The instructions for doing that are found in Chapter 2. If you'd like to tackle the project of making a menorah, check the information on page 40 for ideas about how to do this. Perhaps you'd like to make special placemats as a family gift that can be used at a Hanukkah meal. Use drawing paper that you decorate with permanent markers. If you like to draw or paint, try a picture that tells part of the struggle that led to the beginning of Hanukkah.

If giving presents is a part of celebrating Hanukkah for you, then use your imagination to think of presents that people would be pleased to receive and that also honor the celebration in some special way. The possibilities are endless.

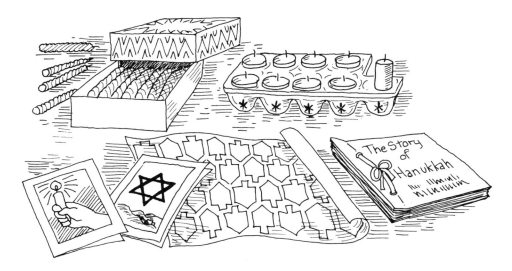

WHAT ABOUT CHRISTMAS?

It would be hard to be in the United States during the month of December without being affected by Christmas. Before Thanksgiving, you start seeing signs of Christmas in the stores, you hear about it on the radio, you read about it in magazines and newspapers and see shows celebrating it on television. Though Christmas, for Christians, is a religious holiday, in some ways it has become a national holiday. It's a hard one to ignore, and the glitter of Christmas is attractive, even for people who aren't Christian.

This book is about Hanukkah, not about Christmas. There are no historical or religious reasons to connect the two holidays. But it turns out that they both come at the same time of year. Sometimes, they even come on the same day. Both are holidays when families celebrate together, enjoying special meals, singing songs, exchanging presents. And, even though the two holidays are very different from each other, there are some reasons why they need to be thought about together.

How to deal with Christmas is a touchy question for many Jews. That's because it's a question that reaches people's inner feelings, often in a deep way. It's important to understand that feelings are not right or wrong—they're personal reactions to situations and experiences. One thing is for sure: People's feelings differ. They always have; they always will. On the issue of Christmas, it's a fact that there are different feelings among people. Christians differ in the ways they celebrate Christmas. Jews differ in the ways they include or don't include Christmas in their lives.

CHRISTMAS FOR JEWISH FAMILIES

There are some Jewish families who celebrate Christmas as well as Hanukkah. The Hirschhorns are one. They celebrate Hanukkah, lighting the candles each night. Gary, Larry, and Andrew receive presents the first night, usually Hanukkah gelt. They celebrate Christmas, too, by opening presents on Christmas morning and going to their grandparents' house for dinner.

The Gottfried family also celebrates Christmas. "We have a tree," Jay writes, "and we open presents that night, but altogether we don't take Christmas heavily. We take it lightly."

Neither family feels that celebrating Christmas makes them any less Jewish. These families' celebrations are not connected with the religious aspects of Christmas. They respond to those parts of Christmas which are visible to everyone—the songs, the decorated trees and lights, men dressed as Santa Claus in department stores and on the streets, the advertisements.

These boys have all been raised as Jews, receiving religious education. Gary, Larry, and Jay have been bar mitzvahed. (Andrew will be when he's old enough.) They've also been raised as Americans. And, as part of being American, they fit some aspect of Christmas into their lives.

There are some Jewish families who don't celebrate Christmas, who wouldn't dream of doing that. For Hanukkah, Joan Singer's family does a great deal—lighting the candles, singing several different songs together, dancing Israeli dances, playing dreidel. Her family—like many other Jewish families—feels that there is no reason to celebrate Christmas in any way. Yes, they are Americans, and follow many traditions of the United States. But they are not interested in celebrating a holiday that they feel has no connection to being an American if you are not also a Christian.

Some Jewish families don't celebrate Christmas, but they experience the holiday in some way. Lynn Rabin's family is one example. They do not celebrate Christmas in their home, but Lynn writes: "I do go to my friend's house and I help decorate their tree. Every year they have a party and my family is invited and we go."

There are families where part of the family is Jewish and part isn't. That's true of Rachel Broudy's family. To celebrate Hanukkah, Rachel's family lights candles. She and her brother, Oliver, share that tradition. They get Hanukkah presents, just on the first night, and Rachel makes presents for her parents and her brother. Rachel writes: "I think Hanukkah is important because I am half Jewish and I think everyone must remember that long ago time when the Jews were fighting. I think Jewish people need Christmases, too. We celebrate Christmas like any Christian family would."

Eve Larner's father is Jewish; her mother is not. They celebrate Hanukkah by retelling the story, lighting (and making) the Hanukkah candles, eating potato latkes, and playing dreidel. They sometimes invite their non-Jewish friends to dinner during Hanukkah to share their celebrating. Eve writes: "We send little Hanukkah presents to my non-Jewish friends and they have fun celebrating with us. They like it. We also get Hanukkah cards in the mail from non-Jewish friends because they know we celebrate Hanukkah." But the Larners also celebrate Christmas in their home. Eve explains how: "We have Christmas stockings and we get Christmas presents from relatives. But we don't go to church and we don't have a Christmas tree. I like the way my family celebrates Hanukkah and Christmas."

THE CHRISTMAS ARGUMENTS

You've just read some of the different traditions families follow. These reflect the importance of Hanukkah and Christmas in their lives. The place that Hanukkah and Christmas take in your life has probably been decided by the grown-ups who care for you most closely, your parents. And what they have decided probably has something to do with their experiences growing up and with what your grandparents had taught them. Your grandparents were influenced by their families and so on.

Many arguments have been made about the Christmas question. Examining these points of view can help you better understand your own feelings, your family's feelings, and other people's feelings as well.

◆ ARGUMENT NUMBER ONE ◆

It is absolutely ridiculous for Jews to celebrate Christmas in any way. The reasons for celebrating Hanukkah stem from a long and difficult struggle by Jews to retain their religious freedom, to remain Jews even in a mixed society. That struggle wasn't only one of Jews against non-Jews. An important part of that conflict was the struggle among Jews who had different opinions.

There were some Jews at that time who were perfectly willing to become part of the Greek way of life. These people thought that struggling for the right to be Jewish was unimportant—even foolish. There were other Jews who were horrified at the thought that the people who were leaders in government—Jews such as Jason and non-Jews such as Antiochus—would dare insist that Jews could no longer live their lives by their religious beliefs. The result of the long struggle was the victory of the Jews for their religious freedom. And, in this light, celebrating Christmas, a Christian holiday, is directly opposite to the spirit and meaning of what the Hanukkah struggle was all about and what it means to be a Jew.

◆ ARGUMENT NUMBER TWO ◆

It is ridiculous to ignore Christmas. Living in the United States means that Jews are not only Jews, but Americans as well. It has so many aspects that are not religious at all and have no direct connection with Christianity. Taking part in it causes no threat to the right of Jews to live their lives as Jews. Christmas has become a holiday in this country when everyone gets into a spirit of giving, of remembering people you often ignore in the rush and pressures of life during the rest of the year. It's full of traditions that are festive, joyous, and appealing to children. It is pointless to pretend Christmas isn't important when it seems to have taken over the entire country. There's no harm in celebrating Christmas. Besides, it doesn't have to detract from Hanukkah, so why not have the best of both worlds?

◆ ARGUMENT NUMBER THREE ◆

Jews should feel perfectly free to celebrate Christmas. Wasn't the struggle that led to Hanukkah a struggle for the right to religious freedom? Besides, if you don't celebrate Christmas, you're doing children a disservice in two ways. One is that children will feel cheated and left out of a celebration that takes over the entire country and most likely the lives of some of their friends. There's no need for children to feel this way.

The second way you'll be doing children a disservice by not celebrating Christmas is that then they'll just see Hanukkah as a Jewish replacement for Christmas, as a substitute. Some children have even said that they like it better when Hanukkah comes right at Christmas time, rather than much earlier in December. It's as if when Hanukkah comes closer to Christmastime, they feel less as if they're being left out.

Christmas is too big to fight, so why not accept it and celebrate it also? It's not a religious betrayal. In fact, for many Christians, a great deal of the holiday isn't tied to religious beliefs, but has become part of the country's way of life. Celebrating Christmas doesn't mean being any less proud of being Jewish. It's a way of removing a distraction and making it possible for Hanukkah to stand firmly in its own right so it can receive the importance it deserves. Celebrating both avoids the possibility of having the two holidays blend into one heap and therefore not celebrating either very well.

◆ ARGUMENT NUMBER FOUR ◆

Celebrating Christmas is no way to face the strong attraction of the holiday. It's true that Christmas is everywhere during December, and for months before that. You can't ignore it, sticking your head in the sand as an ostrich might. But you don't have to deal with it by giving in to a celebration that has no meaning to the lives of Jews.

Talk about the holiday, especially with children, so they can learn about the importance of Christmas to people who follow the Christian religion. Talk about the many Christmas traditions so children can see what the basis for Christmas is and how traditions help Christians celebrate this holiday, just as Jews have certain traditions that help make Hanukkah meaningful.

All that children see are those parts of Christmas that show out front—all the decorations, Christmas trees, department store Santas. Probe the deeper questions about Christmas. Ask a Christian friend for help if you need it. But don't give in to bringing Christmas into your home. That seems to take away from the pride of being a Jew and of celebrating those holidays that have shaped your life as a Jew.

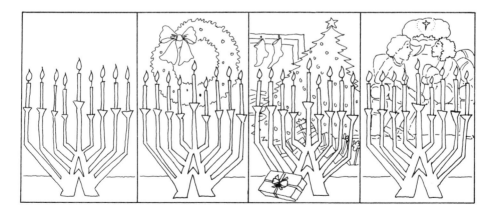

WHAT DO YOU DO WHEN SOMEONE ASKS "WHAT DID YOU GET FOR CHRISTMAS?"

Many non-Jews believe that everyone celebrates Christmas. Christmas, for them, is just a natural part of life and is not seen as a personal choice. There are some things in your life that you treat this way—things you take so for granted that you assume they're part of everyone's lives. Television may be an example. Most households in this country have at least one television set; almost half have more than one. Yet there are some kids who grow up without TV, often because their parents have chosen not to have one. Think about foods. For many people, a fresh bagel is delicious to eat. Many people in the United States, however, have never even heard of bagels. It's hard to realize that something that is such a natural part of your life might have nothing to do with someone else's, even if it's a friend of yours.

So when you come back to school after vacation and someone in your class asks you what you got for Christmas, what do you do? If you celebrate Christmas, this question may pose no problem. If you don't celebrate Christmas, then answering the question may be trickier. The person who asks may just be making conversation. But the question reveals a lack of understanding about you, perhaps, or about the Jewish way of life. What do you do?

Here are some possible answers:

Some kids have answered that question this way:

> I don't get Christmas presents;
> I get Hanukkah presents.

What does that answer really say? In one way, it can be looked at as saying this:

> I'm Jewish and that means I don't celebrate Christmas. But there is a Jewish holiday that comes around the same time as Christmas every year that has an important story about Jews behind it. It's called Hanukkah, and to celebrate Hanukkah we do lots of things. One of those things is exchanging presents. Would you like to know what presents I got for Hanukkah?

Now this is quite a mouthful to say. Lunch could be half over before you get through. But is the short-cut answer really enough of an explanation? Saying:"I don't get Christmas presents; I get Hanukkah presents," may sound all right to you. You may see it as a way of explaining that being Jewish means you don't celebrate Christmas. Or you might mean that being Jewish doesn't mean you miss out on presents.

You may feel you don't want to make a big deal about the question. It was probably asked not to make you uncomfortable but because the person wanted to tell about what he or she got for Christmas. What's important is that you answer in some way that feels right to you and does an honest job of dealing with your feelings.

Maybe you can think of such a question as an opportunity to let someone know more about you. Remember, people are different. One way they're different is based on their backgrounds. Being Jewish is different from being Christian. This doesn't mean you're different in every way—you're both Americans, you're both in the same class studying the same subjects, maybe you both ride a bike and like the same foods and play soccer. But you're different in some ways, and the more you understand others' differences, the more thoughtful you can be in how you treat each other.

THE DECEMBER OPPORTUNITY

There's a big opportunity during December, both for you to expand what you know about Christmas and to help others expand what they know about Hanukkah. Discuss these suggestions with your family, to see what you might add to your life this December.

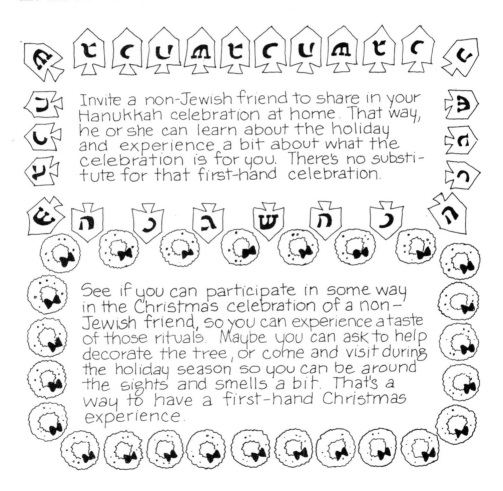

Invite a non-Jewish friend to share in your Hanukkah celebration at home. That way, he or she can learn about the holiday and experience a bit about what the celebration is for you. There's no substitute for that first-hand celebration.

See if you can participate in some way in the Christmas celebration of a non-Jewish friend, so you can experience a taste of those rituals. Maybe you can ask to help decorate the tree, or come and visit during the holiday season so you can be around the sights and smells a bit. That's a way to have a first-hand Christmas experience.

Learn about the story of Christmas if you don't know it. Maybe a friend can share the information, or check in the library for a book. The more you understand about the reasons for celebrating Christmas the more you may be able to understand your own and your family's feelings about it.

If you have a non-Jewish friend who doesn't understand about Hanukkah, tell him or her the story. Explain how the lighting of the candles is done. Tell about what special things your family does. Teach the dreidel game.

ONE LAST THOUGHT

For Joan Singer, Hanukkah is a time "to remember what happened to our ancestors." Lynn Rabin likes "getting together with family and friends, having a fun time sitting around a fire and talking about a long time ago and what the Jewish people had to go through."

You might ask your parents and grandparents how they celebrated Hanukkah when they were younger. What do they remember about the lighting of the candles, playing dreidel, eating potato latkes, or about any other special festivities? Learning about their experiences may help you understand more fully the traditions of your family.

Traditions do change. Remember that potato latkes had nothing to do with the original story of Hanukkah. Using wax candles has become traditional for Hanukkah menorahs, even though in the time of the Maccabees there were no wax candles, only oil lamps. The tradition of giving presents began with the custom of giving money and has expanded to giving other gifts as well for many families.

Not everyone follows the same traditions in exactly the same ways. Traditions are personal choices that have to do with feelings. The story about Hanukkah describes what happened at that time, telling why Hanukkah is celebrated. The traditions provide the ways to show your feelings about that victory. Understanding whatever traditions you follow is important. It's through them that you learn to understand the meaning of Hanukkah and its place in your life.